our song will rise

Medleys of Hymns
with Contemporary
Worship Songs for
the Church Pianist

Mary McDonald &
Bethany K. Smith

Lorenz

A Lorenz Company • www.lorenz.com

Editor: Larry Shackley
Cover Design: Kate Kimble
Music Engraving: Linda Taylor

ISBN: 978-1-4291-3182-7

Foreword

What a joy it has been to collaborate – mother and daughter – on this book of "blended" arrangements for the church pianist. Expressing our worship through music is our gift back to God, and we are blessed to be able to thank, praise and glorify Him with the skills He has given us. True worship has been a vital part of our family for generations, unhindered by changing styles of church services and music. Through a harmonious blend of traditional hymns and contemporary choruses, we have found unity in the message and symmetry in the rhythms and melodies to join in one collective praise offering. From the traditional melodies that anchor our foundation through song, to the ever-evolving contemporary expressions of worship, both seek to profess what God has done and offer promises of what is yet to come.

Each arrangement is the product of two hearts within one family coming together with one passion for a loving God; a God who is Sovereign and worthy of every note we offer up to Him in praise. May the spirit of unity through this endeavor bridge the hearts and minds of those who hear the greater message –that we serve an everlasting God to whom our songs will rise!

–Mary McDonald and Bethany K. Smith

Contents

Forever
with Joyful, Joyful We Adore Thee

Chris Tomlin
Arranged by **Bethany K. Smith**
and **Mary McDonald**
Incorporating ODE TO JOY
by **Ludwig van Beethoven**

Duration: 2:00

LT

4

Blessed Be Your Name
with Blessed Be the Name

Matt Redman and Beth Redman
Arranged by Bethany K. Smith
and Mary McDonald
Incorporating BLESSED NAME
By Ralph E. Hudson

Duration: 3:00

LT

Ancient of Days
with Immortal, Invisible

Jamie Harvill and Gary Sadler
Arranged by **Bethany K. Smith**
and **Mary McDonald**
Incorporating ST. DENIO
Traditional Welsh Tune

Duration: 2:15

O Praise Him
with All Creatures of Our God and King

David Crowder
Arranged by **Bethany K. Smith**
and **Mary McDonald**
Incorporating LASST UNS ERFREUEN
from *Geistliche Kirchengesänge*, 1623

Moving forward ♩ = 120

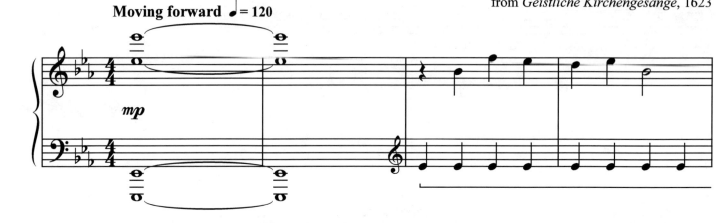

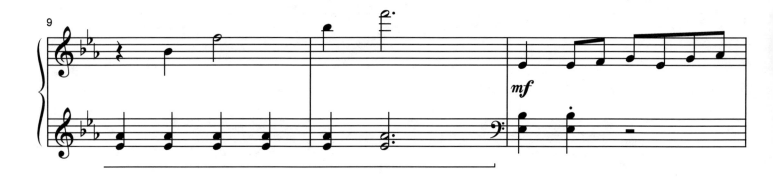

Duration: 2:30

Revelation Song
with Holy, Holy, Holy

Jennie Lee Riddle
Arranged by **Bethany K. Smith**
and **Mary McDonald**
Incorporating NICAEA
by **John B. Dykes**

Duration: 3:15

The Heart of Worship
with O Worship the King

Matt Redman
Arranged by **Bethany K. Smith**
and **Mary McDonald**
Incorporating LYONS
by **Robert Grant**

Duration: 3:15

to Aidan and Addy

How He Loves
with O, How I Love Jesus

John Mark Macmillan
Arranged by **Bethany K. Smith**
and **Mary McDonald**
Incorporating O, HOW I LOVE JESUS
Traditional American Melody

Duration: 2:30

Mighty to Save
with Jesus Saves

Reuben Morgan and **Ben Fielding**
Arranged by **Bethany K. Smith**
and **Mary McDonald**
Incorporating JESUS SAVES
by **William J. Kirkpatrick**

Duration: 3:30